E SAME AUTHOR

d Rebel Chief: The Life of James
th
nting
rdian Field Sports from Old

ts and Huntsmen (3 vols)
f a Cavalry Horse
est Horse Stories
est Dog Stories

BY T